Ordinary
Othe

By the same author

Poetry Introduction 7
Faber and Faber

Steel Horizon: North Sea Poems
Incline Press

JONATHAN WONHAM

Ordinary Others

With illustrations by
SUZANNE SMITH

Drizzle-Dazzle

First published in 2020
by Drizzle-Dazzle
105 Benslow Lane
Hitchin, Herts SG4 9RA
UK

Poems © Jonathan Wonham 2020
www.jonathanwonham.com

Illustrations © Suzanne Smith 2020
www.saatchiart.com/account/artworks/509731

ISBNs
Hardback 978-1-8382880-1-3
Paperback 978-1-8382880-0-6

Printed and bound by 4edge Limited, UK

Contents

Irene Myers

Irene Myers was always a good friend to her neighbour Doreen inseparable in this life you might say like a pair of kids most days in the kitchen sipping tea eating biscuits sharing secrets you might say they were intimate Irene Myers and her friend a meeting of minds they had a special kinship especially in the mind of Irene Myers perhaps the most devoted of the pair she adored her friend relied on her company so when unexpectedly it happened Doreen passed away one bright Saturday morning Irene Myers felt her neighbour's spirit come into her all of a rush it fair knocked her flat she knew her friend had died right then and there but her spirit had stayed on earth in the body of Irene Myers all the hopes and fears of her neighbour's spirit now residing inside Irene Myers the body of Doreen was cast away but her soul had decided to stay most unfortunate or was it fortunate but anyway most uncanny Irene Myers took on the voice and mannerisms of her friend spoke just like her it was most strange that voice coming from an entirely other place it was shocking to anyone who knew Irene Myers to hear another voice in place of her own a kind of ventriloquy even the lady at the corner shop noticed it there was unfinished business but what was it that held her spirit here Irene Myers still had some role to play in her neighbour's final departure from this earth but how many weeks would this go on at night-time Irene Myers lay in her bed listening to her neighbour talking there were things she'd never said in all those years together in the kitchen secrets and threads she rattled on it was Irene Myers' daughter who thought to call a medium a meeting was arranged she came one afternoon in March a shady unlit room where Doreen spoke through the open mouth of Irene Myers and with some coaxing explained that she Doreen had given up an accidental son that's what she said this son so far unknown to Irene Myers or so she said and Doreen's spirit could not quit this earth until she saw her offspring given up at birth and never seen again outside the sky a dirty grey the double-glazing blown the drapes grown tired the medium spoke in kindly tone to the haunted spirit inside Irene Myers telling her she was free to visit her son to make peace with him and depart from this earth Irene Myers blinked twice her friend had gone as quickly as she'd come she had let go of her she had stepped out of her at last.

Ali Ben Am

There's no kind girl for Ali Ben Am there's no girl of his
kind for the gentle Ali Ben Am no girl of his imagination
no girl like his sister no girl like the mother of Ali Ben Am
not like the girl in the office the girl in the restaurant the girl
at the gym of Ali Ben Am but most of all not like the girl in
the posters the girl in the magazines the girl in the movies
of the bored Ali Ben Am wracking his brains thinking
thinking of every girl known unto him this Ali Ben Am
searching searching for one kind girl in the head of himself
the head he carries round on his shoulders the head where
he finds all along she was waiting for him the little face
inside the head of Ali Ben Am that one day is hardly there
and then is constantly there and speaks to him in dreams
and asks him why gentle Ali Ben Am is the movie watching
Ali Ben Am of expanding waist of life going to waste and
so grows in the mind of Ali Ben Am bigger and bigger Ali
Ben Am bigger and bigger Ali Ben Am must do something
must contact her must make a phone call must make a visit
must make a proposal and to the surprise of Ali Ben Am
the phone call pays off the visit pays off the proposal pays
off and though the distance of Ali Ben Am is real enough
it does not seem to turn her off the kind girl no longer in
the head of Ali Ben Am not quite the girl that was in

the head not quite the memory not quite the dream of Ali
Ben Am but at least a girl for Ali Ben Am and a girl for a
wedding and a girl for a visa and a girl for the contract
signed by the hand of Ali Ben Am the gentle shaking hand
of Ali Ben Am who is living a dream in his life who cannot
wake up from the dream of the life of Ali Ben Am from the
life of the girl of Ali Ben Am who has her own dream
beyond the life of Ali Ben Am with the man of her dreams
who is already known to the girl of Ali Ben Am who grows
big in the empty days of the girl of Ali Ben Am who must
pop and pop again the bubble in her mind with talk of
breasts and silky skin in the computer of Ali Ben Am who
is not such a fool who collects the evidence who tries to save
Ali Ben Am from the girl of the dreams of Ali Ben Am who
revokes the familiarisation courses the visa the contract of
the girl of Ali Ben Am who buys a return ticket who files a
friendly severance who fights in court the martyred Ali Ben
Am because even the mother even the sister of Ali Ben Am
do not believe him when they hear the claims of the dream
girl of Ali Ben Am the gentle Ali Ben Am he does not
deserve this in his worst dream he does not deserve this the
gentle Ali Ben Am.

Dawn Dwyer

The big day fell on a Thursday and Thursday fell on Dawn Dwyer as she leant on the kitchen sideboard all of a clatter it fell the way a drawer of cutlery pulled out too far can fall except there was no cutlery there was no drawer there was just Dawn Dwyer by herself in the kitchen leant against the kitchen sideboard trying to resist Thursday falling on her trying to hold up Thursday as houses outside try to hold up their rooves and trees hold up their leaves and Dawn Dwyer was trying to leave and hold up her head she was trying to hold up her shoulders but Thursday was pushing down on her and disaster teetered like a drawer of cutlery a weight that was supported but to which point of being extended suddenly would fall and Dawn Dwyer was failing to hold up Thursday by herself against the kitchen sideboard tears rolling down her cheeks and falling onto the sideboard the way rain rolls down the window the way cars roll down the street the way Thursdays roll around for Dawn Dwyer supported but to which point the roof above her head the cutlery in the draw the kitchen sideboard trying to resist as disaster teetered and the cars rolled down the street all going lopsided as she waited for the voice again with its note of command like a

rattled drawer like a rattled sky Dawn Dwyer pushing down on the kitchen sideboard lifting her head and turning a little enough to see that he was standing blocking the light like a tree blocking the light a house blocking the light the voice with its note of command coming around suddenly asking what day did she think it was did she have any idea did she know it was Thursday Dawn Dwyer knew it was didn't need to be told it was wouldn't support it any longer wouldn't support another day wouldn't support this voice any longer Dawn Dwyer pulling the cutlery draw all the way out letting the silver scatter across the floor the way leaves fall from the trees the way rain falls from the sky Dawn Dwyer felt the weight go felt the weight in her arms go followed her legs out into the light hall followed the hall out into the wet street Dawn Dwyer lifting her head to the scattering silver drops lifting her shoulders for the weight had dropped it might be any day it might be any week she didn't have a clue she didn't think of him she had no roof above her head there was no tree to block the light the silver draw was empty now the empty cars rolled down the street the silver tears rolled down the cheeks of Dawn Dwyer.

Fred Friesla

Fred Friesla looked into a book as if it were a mirror he saw characters that were acting behind his back some of whom Fred Friesla recognised when he looked in a mirror and saw a different Fred Friesla looking back it was a fact that Fred Friesla had confused mirrors and books he had confused the characters in books with the characters in life Fred Friesla looked to find his own face and the face of humanity in books and identified in a confused way those he discovered and those with whom he had daily intercourse Fred Friesla had confused intercourse once a month in the upstairs flat of a philosophy student with a description of intercourse in a book Fred Friesla had read she was a philosophy student who liked nothing more than to have sex and discuss afterwards why some teenage girls like horror and Fred Friesla also liked to have sex once a month and it so happened he identified the philosophy student very much with a girl in the mirror or book as we shall call it that had also been made into a film with a girl who perfectly mirrored the girl in the upstairs flat and was prettier than his imaginings based on the book which is why Fred Friesla found the plain student of

philosophy prettier than he had first considered her having intercourse reasonably often but not too reasonably often a fact which brought Fred Friesla up short when he realised that the character in the film who had intercourse with the girl with whom Fred Friesla associated his philosophy student and about whom it was written that he sometimes danced naked with the girl in the mirror of her apartment in such a way that the old neighbours opposite could see a thing they'd normally only see in a book or a film and with whom Fred Friesla now very much compared himself to the extent of dancing naked in the mirror or book as we shall call it or film as the old neighbours saw it with a girl he considered rather plain very often treated women in an unreasonably controlling way leading them a merry dance with all kinds of unexplained schedules and scenes a characteristic in himself he would never have identified unless he had seen himself in the mirror of a film based on a book Fred Friesla had been forced to put down after his girl found a new boyfriend equally confused by the question of why some teenage girls like horror or at least good at pretending he was after sex.

Melanie Smith

thats my name melanie smith and thats hers 2 melanie don't foget theire exactily spelt the same im aslo a awsome singer exactily tha same as her but my mom that cow wont let me post a vid on you tube as much as i want 2 so 4 the moment im jus a name the name is melanie smith and it kinda freaks me out that sombody sings that and that i sing that and that she has the same name melanie as me is freaky but verry cool and i am hopping 2 post 2 vids on you tube verry soon if u just search on melanie smith and that mikes me so happy that u would search 4 the other melanie and i hayve exactily 50 songs in my song book all the songs of melanie smith and theire verry good and none of them is called northern star but if u give it a fought melanie says goodbye to showbiz with what yore looking at in this song she re-creates herself in her solo career and she did it finally and now she looks so incredibly beautyful she doesnt show her skin like the others and me 2 im not like the others cos melanie smith is just melanie smith called that by someone who dozen care if any 1 lissens 2 me that cow who wont let me post a vid now or ever if she has her way but 1 day soon she cant stop me u can google

me melanie smith youll find a girl who doesn't show her skin and jus proves it with her voice and dancin 2 get away and syay goodbye to skool and slut frenz who don't care if they work in poundland i kno its not easy 2 be melanie but she is so awsome she jus keeps fighting just like melanie smith is goin 2 keep fightin she is my inspirition she jus keeps changin hersell like a lizard changin its spots cos wots passed is passed and jus goes 2 show it was one more phase i suppose even 4 me melanie smith who is so much yunger than her and even if she looks less attractive in what your seeing here her voice is still awsome in this song she did a few on the reunion but otherwise nope shes not doin them again cos shes more girly now and dsnt want to go back to all ways being referred to as sporty thats her own words 2 not literaly but tis what she said I think this song is about opening your heart and I know what she meens im not beautiful like her but im more sweeter like my boyfren says melanie smith yore candy with beatiful wraapping and a good product in it don't forget to gogle me one day im melanie the other melanie melanie smith

Don Cole

Don Cole lingers at the peephole of his mind jangling keys he imagines to pass the time there's a bronze one a silver one a gold one in that order Don Cole isn't one of life's great talkers he stares at the door of his cell a man of hard stares a man of former terror Don Cole is detained at her majesty's pleasure just vaporising time locked up in his mind with moments of leisure he allows to unfold slowed down by pure will it's a terrible error to get caught at his age to get caught after fifty to get banged up for pleasure when he ought to have slowed down put his feet up it's all wrong thinks Don Cole to be locked up like treasure a bronze one a silver one a gold one in that order his mind isn't safe it's been slowed down by pleasures not so guilty ones it's all the same they've taken his gold ring his silver chain his bronze but Don Cole says they can't take his tats the dragon that writhes the bottle marked poison Don Cole an object of her majesty's pleasure not by chance at fifty banged up in his mind with a gold key a silver one and lastly a bronze one Don Cole will pay back in his own gentle measure his mind well sorted and stocked like a

Tesco spending lost time with the dragon the poison the thoughts in his mind Don Cole would not force you for pleasure to drink the poisons of his mind or battle his dragons it's all wrong thinks Don Cole staring hard at the peephole where eyes sometimes pass just a single point not far off for Don Cole one stark measure of fifty years of terror the point of the pain of the pricks without measure the tat on his arm by which Don Cole endeavours to pass the time the long dragon's tail a tightrope to pleasure he allows to unfold slowed down by an act of pure will in his mind drink this he murmurs my darling my sweet one Don Cole holds the bottle to his lips walks in the ring burning inside for the moment of release a single point on a wall not far off that day when he'll slip back the bronze the silver chain at his neck the gold ring on his finger and return to the place of his former longings all he treasured slowed down all those years returned as if by error.

Ella Chun

Ella Chun is a girl you can't easily forget probably taller than you but more fragile Ella Chun does not feel fragile sometimes she feels a little frail a little light-headed somewhat famished she suspects Ella Chun is an individual creation like all the rest probably more famished than you are she comes out on the runway looking confident and tall and not quite sure of her wings it seems Ella Chun has found herself a place where she's no different from the rest though not quite herself in the same high heels and the same body shape part of a summer collection Ella Chun is an individual part of a collection that is different from the other collections though Ella Chun is not different from the other Ella Chuns who make up the other individual collections she is of an unusual but standard shape a shape you cannot easily forget Ella Chun is known for her physique her elegant poise she sometimes smokes a cigarette Ella Chun suspects a cigarette can come between her and hunger and she likes that Ella Chun looks at you hungrily like that you look at her hungrily like that Ella

Chun likes that sometimes she doesn't like that she feels light-headed a little frail Ella Chun sometimes feels she is no different from the rest though she tries to be and why shouldn't she try she gets changed quickly and comes on from the wings in a new dress from the latest collection the new collection different from all the rest the one everyone will want to wear to feel a little like the fragile but elegant Ella Chun she tries to feel less light-headed less fragile than the rest but it is always the same walk and for her the risk of stumbling is no less the risk of putting a foot wrong is what she can't forget Ella Chun is a few inches taller than the norm of girls in high heels she gazes over the heads of all but a few normal girls Ella Chun is no different from the other Ella Chuns who disappear into the wings then reappear in different garb leaving the ever-deepening sensation of one girl like all the other girls shaped by a collection of individual Ella Chuns a girl above all else you can't easily forget and why would you want to?

Douglas Arthur Roberts

Douglas Arthur Roberts feels he has waited long enough to
be with Hilda his wife now in the hands of God and waiting
for him in heaven as each morning Douglas Arthur Roberts
climbs out of bed and onto the shaky exercise bicycle closing
his eyes and imagining himself cycling down the road to
heaven as once Hilda and Douglas Arthur Roberts cycled
through a glen on a summer's honeymoony day of heather
bees and blue sky nowadays he's alone feeling slightly dizzy
sometimes hands a little numb Douglas Arthur Roberts has
some special gloves a special hat a special stick to see him
to the kitchen and since being normally a long time there
making a slice of toast the postie hands him his mail through
the kitchen window or makes a special sign to show there is
nothing today Douglas Arthur Roberts has nothing today
without Hilda who is waiting in heaven wondering what
is keeping him Douglas Arthur Roberts is keeping well
perhaps too well he used to have hot meals on wheels but
now has the frozen week's supply in the made-to-measure
freezer to be taken one a day making space for seven

further meals delivered Monday by white transit to the flat of Douglas Arthur Roberts not quite big enough for the carpet in the lounge not quite big enough for the bed in the bedroom the bed which is now too big though sometimes he is not alone she is next to him saying excitedly how it will be in heaven like that day on the bicycle that day they first met and Douglas Arthur Roberts tells Jack Duffy when they are walking the block and Jack does not say a word who also was once married but does not think of heaven much and can and does do two more tours than Douglas Arthur Roberts does also willing to accept frozen cod or hake most weeks from Douglas Arthur Roberts his made-to-measure freezer needing to be emptied carries it next door in plastic bags his hands a little numb but feels he's helping someone Douglas Arthur Roberts sits in the lounge with her rug over his knees looking at her photograph the carpet turning at the skirting the shaky exercise bicycle hoping he will not be riding it tomorrow unless he is you-know-where.

Camilla Marsh

Camilla Marsh is spinning in time in the evening sunlight she is spinning in time it is quite a moment for Camilla Marsh a moment she'll remember for the rest of her life the big red cherries in the straight golden hair shining in the evening sunlight long shadows falling against the gym wall Camilla Marsh has fallen in line she is keeping in time her shadow and the big girl's shadow dancing together on the gym wall perfectly together in time Camilla Marsh cares only that she's keeping in time in her pink ballet shoes that she is spinning in time watching the shadows on the gym wall and the red cherries in her mind she is distracted looking down at her pink ballet shoes the spinning floor Camilla Marsh dances with a bunch of little girls just like herself their shadows falling against the gym wall this is the way to pirouette says the big girl this is the way to pirouette the proper way I do it all the time says the big girl doing her pirouette for Camilla Marsh this is the way to pirouette and this is the proper way to keep in time it is quite a moment for Camilla Marsh it is quite a spectacle the red cherries in the big girl's

hair stay with her now for the rest of her life the shadows go on climbing the gym wall is shining she looks down at her pink ballet shoes sees the floor is spinning yes thinks Camilla Marsh this is the way to keep in time it is quite a moment for Camilla Marsh her eyes big and pale behind her spectacles following the red cherries shining in the evening sunlight quite a moment she will remember for the rest of her life the shadows quietly climbing the gym wall as Camilla Marsh carefully falls in line distracted by the big girl with bunches in her hair the music rises falls the shadows quietly climb the wall the big girl is the prettiest she ever saw this is quite a moment a moment she will remember for the rest of her life a moment she goes back to in her mind how the music would rise and fall how her heart would spin for quite the longest while this is the way to pirouette says the big girl this is the way to keep in time thinks Camilla Marsh somehow she has fallen in line she thinks of the big red cherries the straight golden hair she thinks of the dusty corner where she was just sitting she will not go back there.

Monday Jones

Monday Jones saw the sunlight flicker up from the great river
below a golden lustre that held the eye it glittered like gold
foil it was the Thames thought Monday Jones the sea reach
of the Thames as Conrad had seen it a historical beast its
muddy banks veined by tidal streams a dark sticky skin lapped
by gold Monday Jones held his mobile in his lap rubbed his
thumb across the screen impatient for his messages below the
aeroplane a cloud was floating as if lost his thumb touched
the ON but did not press he rubbed it back and forth half-
reflecting on something about gold foil an experiment about
particles the gold seemed solid but the particles just passed
through Monday Jones had returned to the city of his birth
he was just passing through there were unclaimed messages
waiting for him in the ether the luminous river pulsed back
and forth its gleaming surface like gold foil now hidden
beneath a few unclaimed clouds the hard-edged dockyards
and magnetised ships the hands of Monday Jones creamy
on one side dark on the other and dextrous as he changed
the SIM card the little gold chip he slipped carefully into

his wallet now the messages would get through Monday Jones glanced over the notes in his wallet the serious faces and the dirty edges of the money in his wallet touched by a thousand hands all knowledge was there in those historical faces printed on notes and passed from hand to hand the plastic cards embossed with gold it all came from down there in the mud the amphibious mud Monday Jones knew that everything came from the mud even he came from the mud as London had once crept up from the mud Monday Jones gazed at the luminous water as Conrad had seen it and the adventurers and settlers and the Romans before them had seen it and the messages he had not yet seen awaited him unclaimed and swarmed in the ether over London the city of his birth soon Monday Jones would set foot on terra firma breathe in the luminous ether he would embrace it he would sink himself into it that is my London thought Monday Jones catching his last glimpse of the sea reach of the Thames its flickering light now passing straight through him like a thousand hands had touched him like he had gold in his bones.

Cindy Spears

It's not like Cindy Spears is the only one half asleep and living in a dream or that Cindy Spears is the only one who can hear in the darkness cars reversing distant voices it's not like Cindy Spears has always disliked the present or could not define herself by the onrush of the present or that Cindy Spears has not sung her own song or that she has not watched her own road movie half asleep with the wall to her back and it's not like Cindy Spears is not starring in her own car with someone who might be her brother or sister lying in the back or as if Cindy Spears is not the only one drinking dishwater coffee at the filling station or refilling the tank getting looked at by the man at the next pump and it's not like Cindy Spears is the only one half asleep and singing her own song a few hundred miles further down the track standing at the filling station pump with the darkness around her and a song in her head it's not like Cindy Spears has never thrilled to a kiss or that Cindy Spears hasn't starred half asleep in her own road movie of a filling station pump with a man in an over-sized car and it's not like Cindy Spears hasn't already asked her brother or sister in the back do they think she's changed because there's no

answer for that and there's no answer for the darkness that is around her or the questions in her head and it's not like Cindy Spears is the only one nodding off half asleep with a portable on her lap and questions in her head the feeble glow emanating at her hotel window and reflected feebly in her eyes it's not like there isn't an empty bed or an empty bathroom for Cindy Spears to star in or that Cindy Spears has not lain half asleep with the constant vibration coming through the wall or been kissed anywhere at all it's not like Cindy Spears has never felt the onrush of the present as she watches some other version of the news half asleep in the anonymity of a hotel bedroom the pillows so comfortable she might be dreaming so many of them piled high in the darkness a pyre on which Cindy Spears lies her head though she can't sleep for the cars reversing the distant voices the darkness around her Cindy Spears lies imagining the anonymous white bathroom it's not like the anonymous white bathroom is an antechamber to an anonymous future it's not like Cindy Spears doesn't feel something she doesn't wish to feel when she goes in there half asleep to push the handle and is grasped by the onrush of the present one continuous roll of paper unwinding and nothing to write with.

Julius Goodfriend

Julius Goodfriend to his tenants Mr Goodfriend to his good friends Julius is to his tenants no friend though he insists on the maintenance of friendly terms at the risk of some incident Julius Goodfriend insists that a friend without patience is not a friend (good or bad) and insists on calling his tenants friends post the signing of a badly photocopied belt and braces contract using his real name Julius Goodfriend many tenants (good or bad) assume that could not be his real name some could not help but laugh when presented with said badly photocopied contract seeing the name Julius Goodfriend for the first time it's funny it does not seem to suit him like that baggy suit he wears with patent leather belt and snappy braces some of his tenants behind their hands behind their rented doors have invented other names for Julius Goodfriend such as Mr Badfriend or Julius Seizer and it's true there is a touch of the Imperial about him those brown weathered hands those gold rings the Roman nose Julius Goodfriend wears gold rings a thick gold necklace has brown weathered bags under his eyes Julius Goodfriend says he is not sleeping well since 'the accident' the tenant list of Julius

Goodfriend is very long it's not feasible to maintain every property to the highest specifications however good relations are maintained on rent day with expected promises Julius Goodfriend rings the doorbell a sharp jab once or twice his signature tune Julius Goodfriend has put his signature to many badly photocopied sheets with endless stipulated rules invented and maintained by Julius Goodfriend but these days since 'the accident' somewhat one-sided the letters he receives from tenants on the one side and 'the accident' of Julius Goodfriend on the other side some would say an excuse the tenants are always uneasy/unhappy/frightened to see Julius Goodfriend politely listen to him complain about 'the accident' which has left no obvious scars on Julius Goodfriend but quite a few on his tenants Julius Goodfriend eventually takes the cheque and swaggers off to his high spec marine blue German car Julius Goodfriend an ex-marine not so fit these days but still able to crack heads (good or bad) if he wants to.

Lindsey Lomas

The camera looms on Lindsey Lomas her flower print dress
a splash of fat a chart to show what each day Lindsey Lomas
takes on after finishing her family's scraps a few more
saturated grammes each day wrapped around a slim girl in
a flower print dress beside a riverbank the sound of children
somehow distant Lindsey Lomas seeming not to notice she
is watching a handsome man reading a book the supportive
husband of Lindsey Lomas somehow distant saying these
changes might not be much fun but he loves her for the
next few weeks each day the total contents of her stomach
wrapped in a film of fat shown to the viewers the inside
facts in daily video diaries Lindsey Lomas records her frank
admissions laced with commentary scraps while off screen
Lindsey Lomas somehow distant is still wrapped up in that
scene the river bank the handsome man the sound of children
was it her the girl with fat on her dress the same Lindsey
Lomas who can't change can't drop the act can't pretend any
more all through the unappreciated fact of her unhappiness
Lindsey Lomas seems in denial to spitting rashers to

sundry scraps adding to the fact that her weight and her family speak plainly of another Lindsey Lomas now required to act before it is too late in this scene which might even be an advert for low cholesterol margarine saucepan in hand flower print dress a splash of fat plainly seen through the camera's zoom lens in the edited version on the stretched screen as one who no longer seems like the slim Lindsey Lomas known from the past who changes in front of her own family almost mistaken near the end for someone else they can hardly believe she reminds them of their mother before the unappreciated fact of her unhappiness left off screen Lindsey Lomas now exercising interest nationwide drops six sizes and drives to the studio where in a bare room she changes in front of her family the flower print dress stands like a child in her mother's best the freshly pressed cotton between her fingers against her back and stands alone before the camera a million eyes and only two eyes looking back along a riverbank the sound of children off screen a few scraps.

Gerry Dunn

When I look at my Gerry Dunn I see a god a body long and lanky those extraordinary hands with dextrous fingers peculiar thumbs I long for them to cup my ears and rub them raggle with me roll me over slap my thighs and rub my tum I'm helpless lolled out on my back upon the carpet Gerry Dunn laughs at me all stretched out so masterful so strong my mind directs his hand across my belly as my back begins to arch in pleasure oh my master Gerry Dunn the fire that crackles biting rain against the window's dark but inside all is love and warmth adoring hands I curl about his feet all night and rise with him first light oh how rejoicing is the shout of 'Rufus come!' I'm at his heels and look up now to see a glow of dawn around his bobbing head my Gerry Dunn my everything my lord a face so oftentimes inscrutable transformed by god-like humours to a face of happiness a face of love the face of Gerry Dunn the greatest father you could ever find the kind you read about in books and true to say he sometimes looks like me the eyes the hair the solid build we knew each other straight away the day when Gerry Dunn came to the home for strays I picked him out my hair

was black but now it's turning grey I scampered then I ran but mainly now I lollop walk I see a sad look sometimes in the eyes of Gerry Dunn twelve years but those were men's years not a dog's yet Gerry Dunn has always stayed the same somehow unchanged still centre of my world always dependable who throws me sticks and rubs my tum always the same grey streaks above his ears the citrus-civet scent I've always known the same smooth reassuring hands that held my head on each of those unnerving visits too bright lights the indelicate prick of the needle I've come to expect it does no harm my eyes are closing now beneath the inscrutable face of Gerry Dunn the fuzzy glow around his head the face I've always loved and feeling now so tired the pain inside going numb my eyes are trying to close and sleepy I try not to close them oh how time has passed a year in a month a week in a day a day in an hour an hour in a minute the face of my Gerry Dunn always the same the face of a god how I worship him my lord my master the everything from which I come I must sleep now I must sleep there is something glasslike dropping from his eyes what is it?

Renata Perry

There's nothing pure about Renata Perry except the pure cries of abandon of Renata Perry nothing so pure as the pure abandon of Renata Perry under the pure blue skies of Italy that Renata Perry can see from her bed the balcony opposite all covered in aerials pointed at transmitters waiting for signals Renata Perry is lying down under the weight of an angel waiting for signals under pure blue skies Renata Perry signals her mouth is dry and asks if he'll be an angel and fetch some water Renata Perry watches him stiffly the weighty angel going stiffly to the bathroom and everybody says you can drink the water it's true it's incredibly pure but Renata Perry stays true to herself and the wine and everybody says Renata Perry might drink all the wine which is perfectly true if not completely necessary Renata Perry might drink all the wine and abandon herself to the nearest angel which of course might be true thinks Renata Perry abandoning herself to her weighty angel and feeling herself spiralling up into the pure blue skies of Italy the balcony opposite all covered in aerials pointed at transmitters waiting for signals she feels the warmth in

which it is so pleasant to make love absently stroking a cheek or a thigh until presently he groans appreciatively Renata Perry appreciates an angel who stands up for himself and usually appreciates it standing up or lying down presently Renata Perry takes it lying down likes to bare her breasts to the angels of Italy and the pure blue skies of Italy Renata Perry loves so much the appreciation of angels standing up stiffly like transmitters waiting for signals under pure blue skies all of them pointed at Renata Perry but Renata Perry doesn't know what she wants between her breasts puts a hand between her breasts puts a hand there or a limb there Renata Perry puts her limbs here puts her whole leg there Renata Perry places the angelic head down between her breasts like this likes the feel of his angelic nose gently strokes the angelic hair Renata Perry is a gift to mankind a gift horse just like the Trojan one a gift horse to mankind her pure cries of abandon behind a hotel wall sometimes leave her a little hoarse but satisfied Renata Perry is satisfied she'll be appreciated for a few more years it makes sense to put her own pleasure first these days her cries are cries of abandon pure cries.

Andrew Lesley

The glass eye of Andrew Lesley gleams in the dark as he sleeps behind the museum glass in the special case they've made for him Andrew Lesley's always been a special case a slip of a man in a heavy woollen coat he looks like a doll or an automaton from the days before television before radio before talking pictures when machines worked on simple mechanical principles understandable even by children Andrew Lesley mechanically rubs his eyes like any normal human would a truly simple man understandable even by children Andrew Lesley doesn't know why life's been so good to him a man who goes on forever who's never stopped the case of Andrew Lesley is a quite extraordinary one he sleeps just like a child his life has been so long it's written down somewhere he can't remember any of it now his head is like a hollow gourd it's good that Andrew Lesley lived so long and good that children come to see him when he sleeps it seems to them the gleaming eye's awake they creep in darkness past the case as Andrew Lesley stares at them asleep the art is good the mystery complete only a child can understand the horror in a

gleaming eye of glass perhaps one day the eye will swivel round and stare inside the head of Andrew Lesley back towards a time when he was young all eyes were glass all minds were part volcanic there were tears abysses cataclysms Andrew Lesley wakes up with a jolt inside his heavy woollen coat inside his special case of glass the empty corridor beyond his eye there are no tears no irritation no perception as the eye takes stock of nothing transfers nothing to the brain it's all quite perfectly simple a child could understand it Andrew Lesley feels nothing it's all quite comfortable no more abysses no more cataclysms Andrew Lesley thus declines his head encourages the eye to fall into his upturned palm the warm hard ball of glass a comfort in his state of mind the blood of Andrew Lesley stirred not merely in imitation of blood it creeps through his body like lava through a forest without fuss his heart has been weighed by the museum curators his other organs too Andrew Lesley laughs at the thought he weighs his eye in the palm of his hand the only part that isn't real the only part that feels real to him now the heft of it.

Biographical notes

Suzanne Smith is an artist she likes art she likes George Grosz Suzanne Smith is a private person she has her own life apart from the lives of others she's not a big mixer Suzanne Smith doesn't mix up her life with other people's lives she doesn't mix her own achievement with other people's achievements Suzanne Smith never said 'I want to be alone' but she might have done though not completely alone Suzanne Smith loves drawing.

Jonathan Wonham is a poet he likes poetry he likes John Berryman Jonathan Wonham is a complicated person he can wear several hats on his one head but Jonathan Wonham has chosen to wear one hat Jonathan Wonham thinks people wearing several hats look odd to him Jonathan Wonham has a new motto 'one head one hat' even though he has a few hats but his brother has more hats or at least he used to have Jonathan Wonham loves writing.

Acknowledgements

'Cindy Spears' and 'Andrew Lesley' were first published in Issue 13 of *Upstairs at Duroc* magazine (Paris).

'Dawn Dwyer', 'Ali Ben Am', 'Douglas Arthur Roberts', 'Lindsey Lomas' were first published in the anthology *Stone Going Home Again* (New Writing Scotland 28, ASLS).

'Renata Perry' was first published in the anthology *The Flight of the Turtle* (New Writing Scotland 29, ASLS).